MEDITERRANEAN MEN

ESSENTIAL POETS SERIES 146

Guernica Editions Inc. acknowledges the support of
the Canada Council for the Arts.
Guernica Editions Inc. acknowledges the support of
the Ontario Arts Council.

NICK MANCUSO

MEDITERRANEAN
MEN

GUERNICA
TORONTO — BUFFALO — CHICAGO — LANCASTER (U.K.)
2006

Antonio D'Alfonso, editor
Guernica Editions Inc.
P.O. Box 117, Station P, Toronto (ON), Canada M5S 2S6
2250 Military Road, Tonawanda, N.Y. 14150-6000 U.S.A.

Distributors:
University of Toronto Press Distribution,
5201 Dufferin Street, Toronto (ON), Canada M3H 5T8
Gazelle Book Services, White Cross Mills, High Town, Lancaster LA1 4XS U.K.
Independent Publishers Group,
814 N. Franklin Street, Chicago, Il. 60610 U.S.A.

First edition.
Printed in Canada.

Legal Deposit – Fourth Quarter
National Library of Canada
Library of Congress Catalog Card Number: 2006923783
Library and Archives Canada Cataloguing in Publication
Mancuso, Nick
Mediterranean men / Nick Mancuso.
(Essential poets series ; 146)
Poems.
ISBN-13: 978-1-55071-242-1
ISBN-10: 1-55071-242-X
I. Title. II. Series.
PS8626.A518M42 2006   C811'.6   C2006-901408-6

CONTENTS

Oedipus L.A.   7

A Gathering of Shades   16

Glances from a Window   27

Oedipus in Smogland   43

Ulysses Reaches the Aeolian Isles
of the Imaginary World   51

The Superior Man   53

New Year's Eve, 1997   60

Mediterranean Men   66

Alexander at Granikos   71

Horace   74

Oedipus L.A.

1

Thebes
spent westward
traveling towards the blinding sun
choking from the dust of foot-traffic
ox and cart, towards the closing
gates, it makes no difference to me

oh Thebes!
sun-whipped city, purple-shadowed
filled with the smell of nectarine and loquat
of lily of the valley and blue-hued iris
eyed and perfumed I, Oedipus, am a blood
flower sightless, eyeless, beyond all loneliness

oh Thebes! sun-whipped city, away from
your ivory walls, your Cyprus cloying to the sense
towards a stony road
lead me

oh lead me, stones, away hurry
towards my sudden turned out heart
withered, dried as the hottest month
of summer towards the parched hillocks away
from this maddest of cities, it was not I caused your
ruination, your doom it is sealed now,

I, following the scent
the tinkling and the bleating of your goats

lead me to the rivers that into the rivers run
far towards the ancient sea
and this angry land, towards that river
away I shall be turned to stone soon
it's alright to be
caught in the glare of your sudden light
I hear the people murmur on both sides
saying, look! it's him! Oedipus, the king!
look!

whispers in the lemon scented wind . . .
oh Jocasta! mother-wife, oh
Jocasta! mother!
wife! oh daughter-sister!
I shall be turned to stone soon
look!

lamp in hand, caught in the fierce
gaze of your blinding light
I have no need for eyes now
though it is night now
and everywhere eyes
eyes! eyes!

I was old before
I was young, destroyer to that
which created me, now destroyed
a murderer of kings now a living
murdered king lost among the clouded
colonnades a white bird
that follows me
(for I can hear the beating of his wings)

at night when the cool of my pleasing what music
shade stops me and I rub my feet
I feel embarrassed to say a clock
is whispering in my chest I ask what music is this
that leads me that I hear like a shepherd's pipe
I ask who is it call me by name
Oedipus, sweet Oedipus, Oedipus,
I remember you, oh now eternal Sphinx,
lucky to be turned to gelatinous stone
for it was I, arrogant Oedipus, who froze you
where is your harsh discordant voice
calling me now demanding insistent your
ether-empty eyes staring straight ahead
you were the horizon incarnate *(you were the*
you were my first love *inaccurate*
do you hear? *horizon)*

it was rage that made me slaughter
infinity creature, man and not you, Chimera,
fear that made me answer thus
made me proud and arrogant
dressed in rags a poor sap with
a cloak that would not close, it was winter

made me approach those men not evil
they thought in their foolishness I
had come to rob them for there were
thieves in those hills
but I was merely hungry and cold
a poor beggar not a thief
and certainly not a murderer
and yet I murdered out of rage

9

I didn't even have a sword
why did you not stop me
you had wings? why not?
why did you not stop me?
and when I waddled out in blood glistening
newborn
covered from head to toe
shining
new and howled my birth rage
among all that slaughtered death
I howled my rage till the wolves came
and the vultures too and picked their
flesh and bones I did not hate
those men but I could not bring
myself to bury them
for three days I sat and watched
why could you not have called me out?
breasted angel, childless, lioness
of the desert, I loved you then and loved
the desert too
and the answer that I gave you
that of man, why any desert fool
could have said
the same and just the same
that all I was, was
a snot-nosed
child, scared to death
who wished to suck the teat
you saw me frozen in that desert wind
and when you saw me
turned to endless stone

oh reason!
bleeding from the brain
it was you reason that led me
to this point
voluntarily led me to this point
and then astounded me

it was you, Sphinx,
with your querulous voice,
strident, musical
a voice of many voices that held
me, you knew the answer
to the answer

I should have murdered you
it was the stake of fear
you held against Oedipus
heavy-hearted and turned my hair white
(just the dust of the secret desert)

oh Sphinx, how I loved you then!
father
father
father
who was it that was left?
it was rage that made me slaughter
(I didn't have a sword)
and murdered all of you

and when I finished with them all
and saw you the gristly one

who died voluntarily
who did so voluntarily
I waddled out all bathed
in blood and howled
my rage, then I thought
I heard the beating of strange wings
why would you have called me out?
I who was left to live
and not to die
in that strange paradise of the night
it was the first time I saw the stars
and held my baby hands out
to eat them like hot sweets

it was I, Oedipus, odious among all men,
who was left to live and
not to die, given the whip and
the embrace of chain, not the dear
caress of Mother and of Mother's milk
the loving sound of paternal affection
no, the all-night calling out to
you, Jocasta, for your mother's milk
and not the venal juice
who would have buried me in that
secret hour my throat ripped out
on that barren hill you snuck away,
the two of you, from the awful sight
and snuck away like thieves
did you make love that night?
or did you weep beneath the blankets
as you heard the howling?
song of bird I follow you

I cannot see but I can hear
the crow that follows me
there are no harpies
just a rocky road lined
with stinging nettles, and skull
bleached blinding rock
I, Oedipus, now in endless flight
brought water to your drought
irrigated the city, could see
as far as the purple shadows of
the mountains there were vineyards now
and fig, olive and sweet-smelling saffron
opened up the trade routes to the north
and east, towards Egypt and far beyond
you exchanged and prospered
but now, oh Thebes!, you line the streets
with whispered gossip and ill intent!
I have always left by night
who would have buried me in that secret hour?
circle torn by the idiot noise
of gossiping men, I cuckolded myself
their king is twice dead and now
I ask who is it shall replace me?

who is that will come to replace me?
what child of the monstrous Sphinx?
you who condemned me in your midst
asking, who is the foreigner come to live
amongst us?
condemned me with your envious eyes
a stranger among you
now closer than you knew

was I blood of your blood?
sinew of yours too . . .
lead me, oh lead me away,
loud stones, from this place, from Thebes,
for I can hear the stirring of her wings at night
a father and a son–brother
to myself, I, Oedipus, who was a king
now fallen from his stay
here by sorrow's foot, that I leave behind
my tears are endless
I could bath the world
and my vision reduced to ash
a single point of light
that calls me out
not one has the right to point
a finger and to say
he was a bad king who didn't care
the blight was lifted
the curse transformed

all else had failed the people
in his need, I loved Jocasta
more than I knew
the circle turns
and returns to point
the wheel that interlocks
the evening air turns and spins
beyond the city gates I hear
the hum of the road
where other men sightless upon the spinning wheels
move through space like rays of light
a time will come when all

such men mouthless, eyeless
will navigate the earth . . .

I go, Thebes,
I, Oedipus, the mountains
to my back have called their longing
the sea and a sweet embrace, their desire
is sent to hillock valley and the stretching plains
and the earth rumbles with earth worms again
cracked and bleeding love
seeps everywhere
and as I sleep and walk
I put forth sudden root!

A Gathering of Shades

I want
to forever find
Ithaca (Ithaca)
here
by the salt immortal sea
I lay down
spear and sword
scabbard and gold-veined
shield . . .
the days of faithful wives
are gone
forever . . . find . . .
the men of winter hold up the sky
I find . . . (find)
the men of winter
hold sway
among
the world . . . today
black angels gather
where I dig
this hole and
pour libations of honeyed wine
my men stand about
sailors all, tattooed . . . frightened
staining the air,
wondering . . . what . . .
what it's all about, this insane

ritual, this diseased journey?

what's the point? leave it, let's go, we're late
dig a hole later in the month, let's go!
into the mouth of the hot earth
late
as it is
please . . . hurry . . . hurry
Ulysses,
please,
Ulysses!
am I
standing
still
barely standing still
among, these dusky whisperings
of dull-eyed interrogative men?
voices, like dry hands, wringing out their necks
like nervous bankers, like frogs, leathery, red-eyed
with worry grown old with worry, dim
this generation of cops and bankers,
tadpoles, uninvolved of real-estate agents
of insurance salesmen! disconnected
I will not sail
with them again
I swear it (underbreath)
I swear it
what's the point of talking to Tiresias

nobody knows who he is anymore
(he's an old man)
he's an old man, tired, blind, for Christ's sake,
he's a stiff with a voice like buttery wings
rubbing together, an afterimage

(where's the first, the identical first?)
of himself
he follows double
then follows after
he's dead . . . long dead
I pour out
clear water and white threaded barley
into the stubborn earthen mouth and will not listen
I am obstinate in my pride
will not listen
I will put an arrow
through the neck of anyone
who resists iron will, taught me that
feather taught to skin to teach
watching the iridescent blood
flow out through the pipe of nostrils
hear the hiss of the air and
the radiant white eyes
shoot back
and I will
pour the black blood of wooly black-eyed ewe
gazing towards the violet sea, gazing

towards Ithaca!
I swear,
stone-pebbly Ithaca,
hill-fragrant land of
how are we to return now to our native soil?
they cry out!
they cry
must we visit pale-faced Persephone
that bitch . . . she's a bitch

they ask, they complain, and push each other
out . . . of the way . . .
a gathering of shades to return the call, mediocre
feeble, sightless old age, seeing the exhausted
dead, here in the hall of Death
I ask, look! look! . . . is she there?
look
long distant memory further than the red-eyed
sun afflicts me, birds
parched with thirst unravelled with time
within sigh . . .
look!
am I to be a shade as well? tell me, Circe! well?
look! look!
transformer of men, liar, deceiver
worshiper of the phallic god
witch and daughter of a god
have I
given up the ghost for this?

am I dead too?
where are my men now
and doe-eyed Penelope what is to be done
about her?
we're not Orpheus they moan softly,
(they make me laugh)
we don't play instruments!
we haven't the talent really
(can't see beyond this dark wall)
we just want to go home to our soft beds, okay?
to our wives and daughters, to our strong sinewed
boys, to our mothers, and grandfathers . . . to our

lapdogs, they moan
far and away, our doors . . . our steps . . . away
from this yellowed isle where the land boils
lard and honey, they murmur . . .
and the stench of death is everywhere now . . .
they cry
Ulysses, listen to us,
we're men not gods
we're not like you
we just want to be comfortable in our old age
have pension plans
and die in our sleep,
let's all just go home, okay?
let's just forget this part!
I won't listen to their weak-kneed murmurs
and stuff my ears with wax
will I perhaps find Ithaca? (Ithaca)

how can I find?
I ask why dare?
it's all movie scores and bad TV toxic newspapers anyway
and processed food, journeys performed
on cellophane skies it's preprogrammed
preprogrammed they say
fights! concerts! dilemmas!
witches! bitches! for what?
for what? for Greece? for Helena?
for that bitch-witch of Troy?
for what?
should we die?
for the gods of Macdonalds?
what does it have to do with us?

we're men not gods!
(and so many men slain, young youths
in their prime, strong of limb
full of Arete, full of spunk
slain lost and for what?
for her?
for Her

it's all tourism, not adventure
wrapped in plastic
in plastic sounds
and sealed bubbled lives
(but the blood was real)
and unemployment lines, microchips
computers to find
cable lines, movies, knives, chips, lice, hand lotion
to find (to find)
toothpaste and headbrushes and advertisements
to find
headrests and critical conditionings of the mind
to find
(destruction of the hippocampus, corrosion
of the anterior hypothalamus and not the liver
and thirst and hunger
and cold, awful cold, and strange beds forever
to find
Ithaca (Ithaca)
and a hard going we shall have of it
shootings in the face and hands, cops, hospitals, police
double sword and scabbard wounds
nicks in the nuts and wallets lifted
in broad daylight in airplanes, bowling

aluminum boats
lethal street drugs cut with strychnine
and stomach-aches and farts and cheap cons
hockey-sports, nonsense, nonsense, the modern
cities of the world, and for what?
Ulysses, for what?
where is Ithaca? (Ithaca)
now
in my hands I grab the golden sail of surf, tear at
and wind-ripped sea, crack open the glass-eyed skies
steer and look towards
away from
an old sky
look towards the black moored ship
and point
to the pole
perplexed to the spleen
pole perplexed, I point
towards the fish-empty sea
and taste
salt-teared relief, empty, vacuous
who am I? I ask, there . . . who are you?
for what do you cry, Ulysses?
as if I had anything to do with starting this war
as if I were responsible for their dilemma
for this, this gathering of shades
these are the words
and the fragments
of word
s . . . sssssssssss
why run away from the blowing, blazing sun
ssssssssssssssssssssssssssssssssssssssssssssssssss

spearward towards the western lands?
leaving behind mother, father, wife and child
oh! and olive groves, thick-footed oaks
I see . . . oh
. . . no eagles on the trunk of this olive tree here
see no augurs, see no perfection
anywhere, on this isle . . .

just frightened rat-like men, donkey men
ape men, fish men and pig men
I see
nothing
no signs, no augurs,
my eyes grown dim like Tiresias
only worse
I need glasses . . . now
how am
I to
return to Ithaca (Ithaca)
to the sweet-smelling land
how return to the perfumed lands?
when shall I master the ways of men
of the sea ways and land ways?
and find (find)
to search the earth-surrounding seas become
a way-finder, bone dry, mud-shuddering
teeth
chattering
word spouting, actionless, lazy, demure, spiteful men
a wall of darkness . . .
surrounds them forever
get away,

I shout, from me
they are
full of the venom of the long days journey
returning want
to find Ithaca (forever)
they are drunk, let me concentrate, I shout
let me concentrate . . .
unweave Circe's spell that has transformed me
though I drank of the sacred herb, though I
found out
her flawless bed and we joined man and God . . .
to find (to find)
is it possible that the swinish
spell circles me yet?
still?
that I don't
understand that
coarse pig hair grows from my head to foot
from head and face and hand forever
to brand me, one of you?
I, Ulysses,
am not one of you. oh . . .
you ate her food, you drank her wine, ate
lobster and champagne and freshly slaughtered game
you lay with her maidservants and now
you want me to guide you to Ithaca? (to Ithaca?)
I am addicted to this spot
unable to return to the starting point
can't you see I am unable to find Ithaca
to Ithaca
forever, to find (to find)
quick

let me look in the mirrored scabbard
is this me? let me see
am I
the one they call Ulysses?
clown-faced feeble . . . dentured . . . old
are these white whiskers mine?
is that me? Is it me forever? (forever?)
should I sail today to the wide-hipped sea?
should we sail today?
it's too late, they shout
it's too late, says the wind, the aeolian wind
too late gurgle the blood chocked hole
too late to find

Ithaca
oh Ithaca!
when are we going now, sea-master? when?
the world is found . . . round not . . . found and flat
how should we get home with no instruction?
with zero construction and zero body fat?
whose white-charged steely eye shall we use?
and by what power?
are we leaving to Ithaca? (leaving Ithaca)

Ulysses, are we leaving?
I, Ulysses, am not one of you!
they cry, weeping grown men, future shadows gathering
(should I lead them to the river of oblivion
for I hate them?)
we all want to go home some day to find
and that's all natural, all natural but
what is natural?

to find?
today, tomorrow, when?
when shall we go home?

oh
Ithaca!

home

Glances from a Window

To my maternal grandmother,
Maria Annuziata Scarfo,
who described human life
as a quick glance
from a shuttered window

1

Music up!

let the flowing wheat be spread!

here was I brought
before your eyes,
oh guurrrnuuu!
oh zanzarruuu!
before your broken image
how perfect is your mirror
let the holy grains cover the banks
for I am thirsty
with want,
with wonder
oh gurrnuu!
many-jeweled one,
many-eyed
four pillared
seven-centered
my tongue is dry
my voice is hollow
guurnu zarmuuu!

here was I borne before your crown!
here was I brought!
how perfect is your mirror!
I am what fish brought
before you, your scales,
many-jeweled one,
before your stone!
(was I brought?)

here was I brought
many lighted one!
putt!
ta!
oh
zazzaruu!
strangers are like friends
oh ptah!
I am what fish brought in baskets
I am what fish I brought
in baskets here by this river
and washed in willow bark
and sulphur-smoked
the gills in sunlight and water
sir, I am what was brought
by water borne by water
born in water
I am what fish is in baskets brought
set before your wooden mouth
and hearing everywhere . . .
I bring tamarind, sand
and honey salt
I bring these things

to these resplendent shores that
you may build a city
with Enki, my beloved,
& of his feet clay!
& of his legs lead!
& of his belly brass and copper!
& of his chest iron!
& of his neck silver!
& of his head and face gold!
with gubb and with ptah!
the light of torch assisting
and hearing everywhere
here was I brought!
oh zazarru!
mazda ahura!
"may the gods who have thrown
me off give help
may the goddess
who has abandoned me show mercy
one who has no god
as he walks along the street
headache envelops him like
a garment
one who has no god
as he walks along the street
headache
envelopes him
wwwwwwwwwwww
eeeeeeeeeeeeeeeeeeeee
oooooooooooooooooo
ah!
on your shadow do I live

The voice
of a
prophet,
inside
that
voice a
hint
of
doom,
oracle.

on a rotting leather scroll!
ah!
. . . there was a beach here once
there was a beach here once
here on this footpath
there was a beach
here
where the goats graze
and up this broken path
a staircase, a temple beneath
an awning of
blue sky and the sound of
everywhere wind

close to the murmuring sea it was
whispering caught between
cloud and Cyprus
and there was I anointed
with balm
and on my skin was placed
a mark between the forehead
and temple between the folds
of flesh
on the right side
beneath the arm
and leather thongs
were
tightly wound
about the calves the
arms
the left foot
was I placed

before your open
wounded mouth
and a voice that
<u>intoneth</u> *(what!*
foot that advanceth!
with gubb and with ptah
the light of torch assisting
and hearing everywhere
here was I brought
on your shadow do I live!
on a rotting leather scroll!

Johnny was in a tavern,
he was lost in a pattern
and he couldn't think why
he stuck out his arm
and he offered me a brew
he said the world is fucked
screw you screw you
Jeannie was baking apples
she was lost in forever land
and she couldn't think where
she opened up the oven
and she got quite a scare

ego ego sum sum
sum ego
ego ego sum sum
sum
ego
in the darkness of my sertap!
aaaaaaaaaaaaaaaaaaaa

through these jeweled eyes
oooooooooooooooo aaaaaaaaaaa

the noise of man
is wearisome
let the flowing grain be spread
like hair upon a scented sheet!
the polished surface of its side
that the hearing makes known!
eeeeeeeeeeeeeeeeeeeeeeeeee

I am swarmed with souls!
I is I
to repeat is I
so am I thrown!
I is I to repeat is I
so am I thrown from fire!
(with water, am I basted)

ego ego sum sum
sum ego
in deo lux
this is the first sin
that of word

2

rain sound
all I know is here, amebic, fantastical
and hearing everywhere, full
amebic, fantastical,
full you in flowing cotton, who brought three
candles, perfumed in the blank halls

and hearing everywhere
the white colonnaded walks
and I am sped
oh your dappled thighs and arms!
nectar has formed on the corners of your lips
like beeswax your forehead
shone
oh your eyes shone!
many petalled
myriad white,
star transfixed
thrown from the big-lipped sea
she said
I is
is to repeat
is I
the full gourd sound
to repeat
in deo lux
is I is i
scrolled laurel
barnacle of skin
skin of blue sky
face of open
loud
to the four pillars of this earth
brown–staunch north
flower–scented south
holy east
holy west
incense lit
on my cheeks

look!
my hair leaps and
burns like waxy fruit
beneath
an angry orange sun
I am
within a white hot flower
in a field of crackling bees
was I placed
beneath you open wounded
mouth
oh zazzaruuu!
oh ptah!
in God's light
and a voice that
intoneth
foot
that advanceth

3

May I be brought back
to life
may the green grain flower
may my heart be sweetened
by a gentle fire
sweet nectar!
may I be reborn again!
though all souls suffer
the travails of rebirth
may I be reborn
with the sweet nectar!
though all souls suffer

the travails of death
and rebirth
may I be reborn!
it was here that this strange bird flew
here that it arrived
wings fluttering terrible
in its length beak open and eyes
jeweled, pearled eyes
open and staring
oh ptah!
oh guurnuu!
into you staring
I was brought
and in your hand a balance
and in your talons a
sword and fire
there was fire and the sound
of everywhere wind
was I brought to this yellow plain
before your giant feet
was I humbled
and consumed
morning sky, pearl sky!
above me
over my right eye
face of bright Jupiter
and Venus
in strange conjunction, the pattern of
the star
in strange conjunction
I thought at first
it was a U.F.O.

at first how strange
that the mind still
plays tricks
at this age
even though
things are now . . .
ego ego
sum
in deo lux
oh ahura!
oh ptah!
one who has no
God
as he walks
along the street
headache
envelopes him
oh Nin
gur
zu!
sun sky! oh beach sky!
a thousand umbrellas
and ten thousand feet
scatter like buckshot
or the screaming seagull
the mountains are too
distant to be seen
here will I build
a temple
with Enki,
my beloved, and the
sound of

everywhere wind
here in this desert
where once an ocean
lived,
here will I live
with Enki, my beloved,
beneath your wooden
mouth
and a voice that
intoneth
foot
foot
that advanceth
will I build your
city I is I
to repeat is I
in deo lux

broken mirror on the wall
broken pattern
of the ocean
am I set before your burning
feet
eyes burning
from your fire
in the city of the smokes
by this empty river
will I grow
oh Gu Ur Nu!
yousaturnmy!
here! here!
oh zanzarru!

I am only what water is
white with glory and with glass
my light is seven-headed
beneath an awning of grass
and seven-starred
there wooden pillars
are

yellow-eyed, frayed voice
a drum has played along this skin
though the oceans
have I traveled
and mountains have I seen
I am only what burnt earth is
still I see the scars of fire
green melted metal
on my floors
where once I stood
proud
I was too proud
distant
not enough
it seems

the noise of man wearisome
though I have been
reborn
countless times
too many times for
adding and subtracting
for division
I have yet to understand one

plus one
I leapt their confines boiling
in my dreams, now
marble am
left alone
not red bricked tower
(here,

a single string is heard,
a slapping sound, then the sound of water flowing
and that they met by this river to intone
that we should not concede to that)

ego ego sum sum sum ego
cotton, the white colonnade

. . . the gills in sunlight and water

and in the blank halls we see
and sulphur smoked
and they met there
and washed in water
and your face shone
as I sang my song of death
before your scales
before me oh lord
broken eyes
broken glances on the walls
broken lives
broken pattern on the glass
oh ptah!
as I sang my song of death

before your scales
before me
oh lord!
broken eyes
broken glances on the walls
broken lives
broken pattern on the glass
as I sang my song of death
before your scales
before me
oh lord!
broken eyes
broken glances on the walls
broken lives
broken pattern on the glass
as I sang my song of death
before your scales
before me oh lord
broken eyes
broken glances on the walls
oh ptah!
broken lives
broken pattern on the glass
as I sang my song of death
before your scales
before me
oh lord!
broken eyes
broken glances on the walls
broken lives
broken pattern on the glass
gourd-sound

gurrnuuu zaarmu!
guurnuu zarmuuu!
here was I borne before your perfect
stone
here was I brought
holy smoke, golly wok o impae,
how perfect is your mirror!
the window is open
the me mirror

with willow thrashing
with demons who are angels
am I
with which I live
you appeared before me
you appeared before me many
your wooden mouth clap
zazazzuuu!
(you have sent me to live here
among these people)
maybe you would have thought that you
had arrived
oh zazazuuu!
oh guru!
put
tah!
by the river of straight steel
in the killing city
slaughterhouse of the innocent
rabbits of despair
I would not have called your name
delivered as

I am now in the hands of
mine enemies where
a banquet had been placed
oh guur
nuu!
oh zazzazuu!

ahura
ptah
in deo lux
ah!
broken mirror on the wall
broken cracks that run
in all the earthquake
directions northeast and south
west towards the endless risings
always more hills
there is a dry spot there
and a wet one there where
the temple had been placed and
the holy place of burial
I will not be found in your
sacred nest
seth of the undertones
in your place of hiding I will
not be found
a men in nomine
broken mirror on the wall
ego ego sum sum
sum ego
in deo lux
among mine enemies

Oedipus in Smogland

1

A homeless man, ragged, dirty pushes a shopping cart filled with antiq-uities over the Normandie Bridge above the Hollywood Freeway. Music up. He speaks.

Alpha!
"the cars circle me about me
they surround me in the four
directions of lost angels
the fool dimension of the desert
world, sweat is on my brow

and I am old, enfeebled, racked
with bitterness, with falling

disappointments, with lack
of essential oils minerals leached by plenty

made colorless
by color, made pain racked by pleasure

the cars dodge me, dodge my dog arf
like mechanical pups
self-contained units of motion

my ripped and filthy throne

to spin me to my concrete grave

to wave me the sirens, I miss me

43

do they not see me? am I dead?

I, Oedipus in Smogland,

racking sob my beard is quite white now

those who carried me

here

on a bier into the land of condos
who spread out my ashes

remember

now my rage
a young man's rage

vitriolic, shaking the fallen!

toothless

trees that you slaughtered,

stupid little man,
that you replanted in your

fearful symmetry
fired to a crisp by a light sharper

than gods snapshot
bigger than the American ream

I, Oedipus in the
U.S.A., garbage man, streetcar man,

no-home man,
will work for food, man,

shopping-cart man, cart

filled with nothingness as my eyeless sight is filled
with nothingness

all-one-world foolishness man
un-man in this culmination of mankind

ding dog arf

(if I could only place
bells on time)
chains on time
and have time
(the goats bleat here)

itself
but time is a thief
for you time thief!

time is

is thievery itself!
(accuse neither the first man
nor the last man of anything
anymore)

accuse you of
nothing anymore
at all
Dong dog

I, Oedipus, am
a blasted man!

2

I am open to your spectrum
temporarily open
to the weave of sound
the awful dust
of desert wind
my face mask-like
theatrical is wet
is dry as drywall
Sphinx, this

and
I am now

open to this blasted weave
that rages about my feet

a shopping cart for a throne
(on this bridge on Olympic Avenue)
in Lost Angeles in this
empty place of a city
empty of place
dee

3

I,
Oedipus in Smogland,

eyeless, toothless, am less
than you

a place
that leaves nothing to
Hollywood

imagination
less
headless
birds everywhere

long-beaked

headless beaked

birds

menbirds
burning
tires in the hot santa ana
winds hot
burn black
thick choking deeds
my heart is light

as a feather, yes,
and fires burn beyond the

straight-lined carceral city
far-vaunted, mouth-fucked

towards the desert cities

of destitution

I, Oedipus,
dooo dog!

(it's always hot here, damn)

and the desert winds pick
up ash and thick smog and blow it
to blackened and eyeless

sockets
racks of plain bad thought drills me

and sends me out then
then out, to radar thoughts

duh to 666

to the world into
the empty places
that leave nothing
to the imagination

I of
of
of a white screen

I, Oedipus,
am an old man
lostman, everywhereman

what

am foolish and forgotten?
I who was
who had a young man's rage
am

I, Oedipus in Smogland,
eyeless, toothless, am less
than

I, lost now, am

am I foolish and forgotten?
have you forgotten who I was?

have I forgotten myself?
am
and have you forgotten?

you, Thebes?
and if you
have forgotten the howling ceremony of intent?
then you
to you

to your
of your fidelities

there is no loyalty to kings!
anymore
there is none
no loyalty to kings!

ding dog

I, Oedipus in Smogland,
I, Oedipus in Smogland,
eyeless, toothless, am less
than you

dong, killed

I, common man,

in came from you
from you
am reduced now below you
dong

Con Thebes Thebes Thebes Thebesthebes tehebes
thenes thenbesthebesthebesthebes thebes thebes

Oh Thebes! Sunwhipped city!

Ulysses Reaches the Aeolian Isles
of the Imaginary World

here as the white-frothed waves lap the
charred wood of the beating prow, and raise

the lip of the purple sea, here at longest sunset
at the longest part of the year,

heading towards the mainland
away from the Isle of winds, away

from the sacred Isle,
the Isle of the Dead, the child is with me

and we watch the smouldering earth, shaking like
ragdolls for we have witnessed the death shrouded

day of reckoning carrying the bier over
the bright yellow sands our feet hot burning our

brows, feverish and the smell of death almost
warm, comforting, in our nostrils

we, who traveled so far from the motherland
carrying the sacred flame, consulting to oracle

for this new him, witnessed the hazy mountains
above the waves, land of springs and wild boar

of mushroom, olive, laurel, thyme, of oak and pine
land thick with juice and knowledge beetle-led

landed on these pebbly beaches and rejoiced
far from out native land, witnessed, shook ourselves

like dogs and set about to claim
this virgin land, a new home a new hearth claiming

a home within our hearts
beautiful as the rest was beautiful

raised a temple on the marchy swamps
dedicating it to the aelian gods and to him

who-carried-us-on his slippery back to deposit
us safe and sound, here, cala...o...oo...oo...bria...bria...

it was raining when we arrived and then the sun
like a bright young pup shook itself and rainbows

fell. it was a day la lala la la hey ho! la la la leyla hey ha!
ha! ha! ha! we shook like timber in the rainfall sunlight

sound of buzzing bee and quercotil, sound of rock and
sunroar in our ears, the ocean shore, the wave big as

elephants hey! hey! hey! ho! ho! ho!

The Superior Man

speaks from devils mountain and other shouts

flying fire-fly dragons in the heavens
return to earth
the sage is given a choice
the hero too
which is it sage or hero?
men come crowding about
the inferior reigns
the superior retreats
the superior man
wise and strong
is crowded out flying
pigs and fishes are everywhere
a sign of the times
what is one to do?
he asks when one is crowded out?
the superior man

keeps the back still and suppliant
retreats into his thoughts
forgets the future and the past
shows thrift in expenditure
accepts the loss

it is in the nature of the times
he knows that
decrease follows increase
as increase follows decrease
he weeps in the sign of abundance!

as increase follows decrease
so decrease follows increase
he laughs in the time of paucity!
what happens to life here
doesn't really matter
he knows this
what is still here is very important
he knows this too

how is one to live? he asks perseveringly
how is one to breathe? he asks, continuously
(for he never tires)
what is it the signs portend? he asks
though he does not believe in signs
sees nothing in augurs or spells
yet is spelled at all times
a divine child sucking at the cosmic teat
doing nothing

when the loud reigns and the
quiet is not heard when the
hard is everywhere and the
invisible is not seen
when the visible is visible
where is the invisible?
the superior man asks

while man sees with human eyes
God looks into the heart
how is one to behave in such times?

a white flower is a white flower

a rose is just a rose yet loss and gain
are just the same, loss, not loss
what's the difference? he asks where's
the difference? what is difference?
he says:
do not throw yourself
on the world
what is yours is yours
that which is not yours is not yours
you cannot lose it
what's the problem?

the devil's country is everywhere
and superior men are everywhere oppressed
how is then one to behave in devils country?
that's the question, what's correct
he looks within, he notices
the northern border has become an alms-house!
for tattered beggars – is filled with malice!
is filled with smoke he finds

and the mirror
is filled
with snakes
and ladders and
filled with caprice forever and a day
then says be careful all day long!

the superior man cries out from devil's mount

the sage calls out
do not gloss over evil!

he calls out
it wears eyes for skin!
it sees the need!
calls for desire!
but evil must be resisted
at all costs

the superior man knows
that there are destructive people
and is thoughtful
(he does not think of weapons)
at night he goes in for rest and recuperation
he knows they come knocking at the door
in the middle of the night
but doesn't lose a wink over it
death comes sooner or later
for everyone, there are worse things
than death, nonetheless
and he is cautious
and makes
energetic progress towards the good
he knows perseverance furthers
hence the added admonition

need is everywhere he knows
great need is everywhere
and where there is great need
great loss cannot be far behind
he knows this

the superior man is cautious all day long
like the old fox he tests each ginger step

but flows nonstop all day long
like water, and is not bothered, does not
hesitate yet he is cautious
what a paradox!
he thinks

there is hunger
there is thirst
there are the seven ignorances!
there are the seven curses!
there are the seven answers!
there are the seven blessing!

the fire shines far, he knows it
there is possession in great measure to find

there is possession in lesser measure
there is the taming power of the great

there is the taming power of the small
in the mall
where is the clarity in the heart of the city?
it matters not city or country
it matters not hero or sage
warrior or true priest

curb all evil he says
be benevolent, be cautious but
do not be fooled by devils country
be blessed by heaven

seal the nine openings!

close the nine gates!
shut the nine doors!
eat when you are hungry!
drink when you are thirsty!
sleep when you are tired!
what is so difficult about that?

when the inferior reigns
superior men are everywhere oppressed
he knows it

what is one to do
Ah! ah! ah! and oh! oh! oh! and final hum!
ha! ha! ha! and oh! oh! oh!
and final aum!

cultivate the personality
the superior man says
keep the back straight and suppliant
find inner calm and gentle perseverance
abide in virtue like a tree
retreat into your thoughts
invite the ancestors to the banquet
the tao is everywhere, the change is
everywhere, be moderate
seek harmony with God
the superior man knows this
and speaks

do not transgress the law of natural development
know how to
ward off unjustified attacks listen

the wild goose draws
near the heights
you can hear her in the stillness
she flies high above the clouds
her feathers can be used in sacred dances
perfect yourself!
the time draws near
know yourself!
the time is now
look within!
do not wait!
look within
unnnh!

New Year's Eve, 1997

New York,11:55, Seventh Avenue
and Fifty-Sixth Street the big headed
cops in black iron mustaches
drink espresso in the steaming
cold, fifteen below and the crowd
swells, the helicopters casting
huge lights/shadows on the
skyscrapers the canyons of New
York the expectant wait its
11:57 we walk into
a red-nosed dinner bar/club it's
160 bucks just to sit down the joint
it is Jumoin, the bouncer, at the front door
says hey! it's 160 for two just to sit
in this part of town
now is now the crowds
a million of them or more
all up and down Seventh Avenue
climb the balustraded buildings
the sirens go hink honk in
big bowl of balustraded lights
and they're hanging from the rafters
the toilets the lampposts the sides of buildings
as b&w balloons search the black cold
skies rising higher and higher
into the chillcold nights
honks of cabs and cars
trucksoverload I saw coming
over the Queensborough

a dead drunk face first
into the pavement and the
hand not passed out he
had frozen himself to death
the waiters from Portugal
and the concierge from France
the divan from all over
it's New Year's day at 12:01
and I think maybe we'll
meditate and read the infinite
harmony the tertrahedronal
squaring of the circle the constant
k and the ratio of pie which
I ordered blueberry but
got cranberry and apple at
the NYC deli the steam from
the underground sewers
it's an architectonic city
one of the twelve navels of
the earth like the twelve apostles
I can't see anymore barely
to read the papers or is it that
I have lost all interest in the
world and I understand it
a paperboy's route this
search for ecstasy ex-stasis
out of body to leave it behind and
float like those newyorknewyears
ballooons higher and higher into
the pitch black chillcold night
I guess it had to be that way
all the words already spoken all the

events already done all the
number of the days already summed
up and completed the paradox of
the eternal recurrent present
this moment this very moment
in the monastery moment's world.
I think of summer and the apple-blossom
days of youth when we ran free
as gizzards into the blankety-blank sunlight
and God was not man and
manchild Christian or otherwise in the
full-flushed dream the swelling thing
of it, it's too much too much
what stupidity and rancourous self-doubt
the system that thrives on cemeteries
and I saw a man frozen face-down
into the nebulated snow and those who
walked by and those who drove by
and he dead on the pavement
from sorrow and loss,
America, the world sees
the spinning orb the sirens on New Year's day
heading towards the millennial dance
in New York City after Santa Barbara
Vancouver Toronto Montecito
Los Angeles Moscow Prague Rome Paris
Bangkok Tokyo the cities the world
the spinning universal state of man
Manhattan Isle of God
bought for a few glassy beads

oh we try try to cry and fungificate
the earth its dimpled sides

the vast oceans and mountains
eating and sleeping
and smoking the body electric
the Brooklyn mountains and
the human hue and cry
as we move upwards towards
the asking price summmons and
subpeaonas and courts looking
for justice and this poor homeless
black madwoman to whom
I gave carbonized food exclaiming
with tears in her eyes freezing
from the boxer cold
oh you do love me! you do
love me, poor woman! that
tear sprung into my throat and
I weep for the common state
of man and woman
homeless and motherless
fatherless brotherless
sisterless childless
and if only the tears
would come, if only I could
cry for all the loss and disappointment of her
and the waste of life and beauty
and the great stainless steel jaws
of death chewing everything up and the
the singing yellow moon high
above the world, the sad yellow
moon above this earth where
we spin spin spin and dance
and love and lose and hate

d fight and for what we eat
nd fight for what we have
and fight for what we don't have
and shit and sleep and talk
and walk and make and
build and for what I ask that we
we move towards the spinning end

oh god of palaces and kings
of paupers and paper planes
of the lands within the body
god of countries
god of endless hope and alteration
god of attrition and the fixed stance
of the inevitable altercation
god of knowledge and understanding
oh god of truth and god of lie
god that creates and destroys
oh god of endless enterprise
god of the spinning wheel
god of the factories and bridges
god of the computer
god of wall street and the
moneyed dance
oh god cross-eyed loving and
lustful that gave us fruit & trees & flower
that made sea and mountain and grass-filled
plain the seashore and the highwind
the sea the sky the moon and sun
and the frightened mess that made
me and you without which
there is no world no cosmos

no stars or no sun
god of alligators
and crocodiles of elephants and
tigers and giraffes and monkeys
and dog and cat that live high
above the understanding
that walks high above the clouds and
in the small regions of the genetic nonono
code that we unravel in our search
for him, in our lookout for
him and he is everywhere
gate gate gate
paraman gate parasan gate
buddhi swa–ha

we in the canyon walk must sing
the fruitless calling forth for we were
born to sing to sing and die and
to wake up once and for all and not
by the gidgeoned dance see the
truth of it once and for all and
stop the nonsense
we're all one
there is no thou no you only
one me I who exists and includes
all that is or ever will be
and hold forth the ecstatic dance clear
the air for once we see wide with purest sight
the truth and what is the truth now in the
unforgotten turning of the year in the
unforgotten turning of the year

Mediterranean Men

my uncle Vince came to Canada
after the war
to work in a factory
with his brother, my father,
and he worked there for
forty years, raising his children
and supporting his wife
on a salaried workman's pay
neither he nor my father
went into business
neither became rich
they took the streetcar
to work every day for forty years
and returned at night by six

after he bought
his own house
and at night after work
in the summer
took a promenade along
College Street after dinner
smoking his perpetual cigarette
blue jacket slung over shoulder
hair slicked back

he had one of those faces carved
in stone with a fixed expression
neither kind, nor cruel
a Mediterranean gaze

an immigrant's look
it baffled me

I guess
he could have been Picasso
my uncle
but he didn't possess the flair
that mad flair people here
in Canada continuously
refer to
full of the god–knows–what–
substance of manic
abuse
but I think he might have been
Picasso nonetheless
one without paints or brush
or the need to paint
the need to impress
he simply did his job and went home
ate his supper and took his walk
along College Street or St. Clair

a rather stillness to his soul
a hunch–sunbaked quiet of the soul

alerted gaze towards the infinite
always a cig in hand, blue jacket
slung over his shoulders in that wop
friendly way, as he walked along after work

this was his only recreation
other than playing a little cards

at the café or the occasional glass
of homemade wine
attending a wedding
or a funeral
I don't remember him
ever coming for Christmas
or giving me a gift but I liked him

he died of cancer at home
spending his last few days on
earth in Canada sleeping
on the couch
a quiet man of few words

I met someone who knew
him in the old country
who had returned after the migration
back to Mammola
who didn't miss the cold floppy
winters, who took those walks with
him in those Toronto summers
when there were still
fireflies on College Street

I think my uncle could have been
Picasso, without paint or brush
having no need to paint canvas
but painting the air nonetheless
with fantastical designs
strange spouting poetry
and those beautiful orphic birds

I miss him
this quiet man of the Mediterranean
his quiet spirit of determination
not grim or sour but like
something that had endured
the end of world
many times over
and come out on the other side
to walk the streets of Toronto

he died two years before my father
the smoking killed him and the glues
he worked with in that factory
by Lake Ontario

I'm sorry I didn't attend his funeral
but I wanted you to know
that I missed him and loved him too
this man of the Mediterranean
forty years raising families
would take
a passeggiata

how
he did it, day in day
out, year in and out,
with no complaint

I remember now
how he would whistle
as he strolled, those soundless
whistles that men

used to make who knew
they were just
passing through
the desire

the magazines
the newspapers
the need
abusive need
but I think he may be

Picasso without that first p
and then the separate i
followed by the collusion
of the rest
casso
Picasso without Picasso

along College Street or St. Clair whistling
back to Mammola in Calabria

an anonymous
perambulator
he could have been Picasso
with or without the brush
walking in and out
of the worlds

when the world
was still separated
by distance

Alexander at Granikos

you wept at Granikos
wept at the site of the
spear-won land
head tilted towards
further conquest

the flute players
tickled your fancy
and when the women
came to make libations
you were unimpressed

what divine honors had you
saved for yourself? was it
the lands beyond Asia Minor
when you walked by the
colonnaded avenue of your
divine city holding hands
with Athena and Nike?
was it the westward lands beyond reach?

June 10, 323 B.C. in Babylon
you died mute and talkative
Roxanne was pregnant
and that mental defective brother
of yours, Arrhidaois, incapable of rule
you gave your ring to Perdikkas
ordered your body to be taken
to Ammon, one-eyed, got central Asia

and the factions, made plans for six
great temples built at key sites
founder indissoluble, now white-marbled
your clouded brow, Leonine,
skopaic your deadly stance
armed with aegis and thunderbolt
with horn and mitra
crowned by Ge, personifier
of the earth itself what eastern
Sarrapin could stand up to you?
Alexander?

in your honor snakes were fed
at the household altars
spear in hand, you were not wood
and stone but realer somehow
in Death's gripped bud so surpassing
in excellence and power as to be
a god among men your tutor
said, son of all-knowing Zeus,
Hegemon, Basileus, Arche . . .

Lion Man
were you?

not performed, and the exchange of
populace between Europe and Asia
not performed
so many plans, your body mummified
protected by two golden lions
so many plans lost
and golden acanthus, and sixty-four mules

to pull your death chariot, spectral,
a golden veil about your face
you sitting upright, splendid specter
in hand, what a sight that must
have been, Alexander,
your sybaritic body
in the haloed lights of twilight

the silver shields stood guard
a joyful hearse announced
your passage to the underworld

what were we mortal men to think
of such a sight?

you always rode into battle first
you impersonated the gods, your titles
endless, averter of evil, in an elephant-
drawn chariot, I wonder what your
tutor must have thought, ruler of the
world, ream-horned, focuser of the worlds

you sacrificed to Protesilaos
throwing your spear
from ship to shore
to receive the homage of the waves
before the battle at Issos
to Thetis, Nereus, Nereids, Poseidon,
like Achilles, your predecessor
abstaining from sex and sleep
ever to be best and excel in all things
for Arete entered the house of Death

Horace

I miss you, Horace, dear friend,
how we laughed
how I
miss drinking wine under the olive trees
at your villa in Capua, lollygagging, drinking
new wine, how I miss the purple-scented
acacia and the buzz of the summer afternoons
we were
just like the sons of Etruscan kings
how I miss you, dear poet,
your fearless dark moods
green fig eyes steady, unafraid, even
of the emperors stealthy needs, his
conquests, his avatar concerns
for nothing
nothing at all

he wanted you, dear poet,
wanted your living spa
fresh as the waters at Vesta
there in the giant apartments of the empire
he threatened your life once
night-drunk on Grecian elixirs
there by the gurgling fountains he said
smashing a goblet against
the marble floors (it rattling)
there! there! he shouted,
do me this, dearest poet; do me this!
there is life, welcome to it!

in life
there was nothing that you could not steal
once it was just
grist for the mill and your lively pen
if only we could see ourselves as others see
us you said that would be happiness indeed
you found hidden wine even in the sloppiest
joint, the driest spring, the lousiest rathole
in twisted taverns and forlorn houses
and in the palaces of emperors
joints you said
they're all just joints
and kings and slaves, courtesans, matrons
soldiers centurions why
they're just a bunch
of old guys

there are songs that can drive off sorrow
you said beware the young women
rich beyond gold and silver
stay away from their charms
be afraid
afraid neither of the sword nor the emperors
sternest glance
but, as for these girls, stay away

you taught and knew
how to live back then
when loves burning fires
dashed you to embers and
charred you
you simply dusted off your rind

smacked your thick African lips
and poured another libation
in the shade of these thick green vines
neither time nor place
will forget you there beneath the
giant fig tree
in the green shadowed
foliage in its cool shadow
shhh, listen! you say shhh!
what difference love or hate?
youth or old age?
what difference?
all is passage!
all is passage!
passage all!"

oh I am
so forlorn, so racked
with pain
so foolish in my ways,
old man,
hard times can drive a man so
insane
splitting your gummy sides
joints splintering on the rack of pain
remembering lost love,
my dear boy, you have a fever
a simple love fever
it will pass
as all things pass
I am become sick
of it

from the loss of you
and what do you want from her?
you ask meowing children? a hot house
filled with toenails? with boiling cauldrons?
dishes? appeasement? what exactly?
is it marriage that you seek?
no less!, to the Emperor himself
I at least have poetry to offer
what have you got? your dick?

no one can answer this today
or yesterday or tomorrow
what can love finally bring?
besides its loss, its final sigh
a final consummation
on a rickety old bed
toothless and gummed
a yawn?

I hold its child against
my chest this child of love
and smother it
with my giant breasts
dash its brains against
the wall
the hell with love
I say the hell with all of them
and break down weeping once again

you've had too much of the old wine
and you look at me with
those green eyes and smile

full of beans and wine
and chicory
full of the bread you have
grown on this land of yours
try the new wine, it's better you say
get a rubdown, that's what you need, calm down,
down, dammit you're making a scene or
drink till your heart drops into
ecstatic sleep and remember
the loving arms of this full
night of summer
forever
make a choice, you fool,
so what if she's married
to the emperor?
so what if she had men
more than one
and will again?
so what if she won't leave him for you?
go to her you fool
and drink your fill,
from her clear well water
what can love take away
that hasn't already been taken?
what can it give that you don't
already possess?
look at the good side, you're neither
slave nor soldier
but at this rate you won't be
a stupid beggar at the door
of the eternal city
what value does love have?

what value
to us today? what value
in our canned merchandised
lives, mixed together with
the smell of rot?
fish in the hallways and chemical spray
the frayed carpets
the preserving marmalade of it, its lick
what's a fuck between friends?
kill passion and you kill
God
kill God and you kill love
kill love and you have nothing
left, the clicking clock
the rotation of a dead
rock, nothing, nothing, nothing
better to accept the boundaries
nature has invented for herself
better to flee, clothes trailing in
the dark night, better to give up
altogether, Horace, old friend,
what are you to do?
how shall you be appeased?
how shall this fire find its
ash?
how? how? how?